Hudson Area Public Library
PO Box 461
Hudson, IL 61748

Surviving History

ALCATRAZ

Virginia Loh-Hagan

45TH PARALLEL PRESS

Published in the United States of America by Cherry Lake Publishing Group
Ann Arbor, Michigan
www.cherrylakepublishing.com
Reading Adviser: Marla Conn, MS, Ed., Literacy specialist, Read-Ability, Inc.

Book Designer: Melinda Millward

Photo Credits: © f11photo/Shutterstock.com, cover, 1; © MintImages/Shutterstock.com, 4; © kittirat roekburi/Shutterstock.com, 6; © Pavliha/istockphoto.com, 8; © StefanSCH/Shutterstock.com, back cover, 10; © ekko81/Shutterstock.com, 12; © attie Steib/Shutterstock.com, 14; © f8grapher/Shutterstock.com, 16; © Casezy idea/Shutterstock.com, 18; © GL Archive / Alamy Stock Photo, 20; © RightFramePhotoVideo/Dreamstime.com, 22; © Inked Pixels/Shutterstock.com, 24; © LuckyU3/Shutterstock.com, 26; © Jemny/Shutterstock.com, 28

Graphic Element Credits: © Milos Djapovic/Shutterstock.com, back cover, front cover; © cajoer/Shutterstock.com, back cover, front cover, multiple interior pages; © GUSAK OLENA/Shutterstock.com, back cover, multiple interior pages; © Miloje/Shutterstock.com, front cover; © Rtstudio/Shutterstock.com, multiple interior pages; © Konstantin Nikiteev/Dreamstime.com, 29

Copyright © 2021 by Cherry Lake Publishing Group
All rights reserved. No part of this book may be reproduced or utilized in any form or by any means without written permission from the publisher.
45TH Parallel Press is an imprint of Cherry Lake Publishing Group.

Library of Congress Cataloging-in-Publication Data

Names: Loh-Hagan, Virginia, author.
Title: Alcatraz / by Virginia Loh-Hagan.
Description: Ann Arbor, Michigan : Cherry Lake Publishing, 2021. | Series: Surviving history | Includes index.
Identifiers: LCCN 2020003285 (print) | LCCN 2020003286 (ebook) | ISBN 9781534169111 (hardcover) | ISBN 9781534170797 (paperback) | ISBN 9781534172630 (PDF) | ISBN 9781534174474 (ebook)
Subjects: LCSH: United States Penitentiary, Alcatraz Island, California–Juvenile literature. | Alcatraz Island (Calif.)–Juvenile literature. | Escapes–California–Alcatraz Island–Juvenile literature. | Prisons–Juvenile literature.
Classification: LCC HV9474.A4 L64 2021 (print) | LCC HV9474.A4 (ebook) | DDC 365/.979461–dc23
LC record available at https://lccn.loc.gov/2020003285
LC ebook record available at https://lccn.loc.gov/2020003286

Printed in the United States of America
Corporate Graphics

TABLE OF CONTENTS

INTRODUCTION 4
STAY OR ESCAPE? 8
BLOCK A OR BLOCK D? 12
GOOD OR BAD? 16
WORKER OR INMATE? 20
GHOST OR NOT? 24
SURVIVAL RESULTS 28
DIGGING DEEPER: DID YOU KNOW...? 30

Glossary 32
Learn More! 32
Index 32
About the Author 32

3

INTRODUCTION

Today, Alcatraz is a museum. Over 1.5 million people visit it every year.

Alcatraz was a **maximum security** prison. Maximum security means having a high level of protection. Alcatraz was open from 1934 to 1963. It held the most dangerous male **inmates**. Inmates are prisoners. Alcatraz held inmates who caused trouble at other prisons. These inmates may have tried to escape. They may have started prison fights. Alcatraz prison was called the "prison system's prison."

Alcatraz is the world's most famous prison. It was home to a total of 1,576 inmates. It held some of the most famous **criminals**. Criminals are people who break the law. An example of a famous inmate is Al Capone. Capone was a **mob boss**. A mob boss is the head of a criminal group.

Inmates built some of the Alcatraz buildings.

Inmates lived under sparse conditions. They only got 4 basic things. They got food. They got clothes. They got medical care. They got a safe place to sleep. They didn't get anything else. They had to follow a strict daily routine. This taught inmates to follow prison rules.

Alcatraz had 3 floors. It had 4 main **cell blocks**. Cell blocks are prison housing units. Alcatraz had an office for the **warden**. A warden is the prison boss. Alcatraz had a room for visitors. It had a library. It had a **barber**. A barber is a person who cuts men's hair. Alcatraz had a dining hall and kitchen. It had a hospital.

STAY OR ESCAPE?

The island was named *La Isla de los Alcatraces*. This means "the island of the pelicans." The island had a lot of birds.

Alcatraz prison is located on Alcatraz Island. This island is located in San Francisco Bay. It's hard to get on and off the island. The prison was thought to be the strongest in the United States. No one could escape from it.

Alcatraz Island is full of sharp rocks. That's why Alcatraz prison is called the Rock. It doesn't have many plants or animals. It's hard to grow life on the island. It doesn't have a fresh water source. Water and supplies were brought in by boat.

Alcatraz is surrounded by cold waters. The water has strong **currents**. Currents are waves. Alcatraz waters were also thought to have sharks.

QUESTION 1

Would you have tried to escape from Alcatraz?

A You didn't want to take any risks. You were scared of sharks. You knew the water was cold. You knew there were dangerous currents.

B You were a strong athlete. You were well-trained. Over time, you found and hid supplies. But you were caught.

C You wanted to escape. You hated being in prison. But the last time you tried, you were not prepared. You got hurt on the rocks. You were caught.

Alcatraz Island was also called "Uncle Sam's Devil's Island."

SURVIVAL TIPS

Follow these tips to survive a shark attack:
- Stay out of shark habitats. Habitats are homes. Avoid the mouth of a river. Avoid fishing boats.
- Don't take your eyes off the shark. Know where the shark is at all times. Don't turn your back as you move away.
- Stay calm. Don't make any sudden moves. Stay as still as you can. Hope the shark swims away without bothering you. Remember, you can't outrun a shark.
- Move slowly to the shore or boat. Go to whichever one is closest. Get out of the water. Don't thrash your arms. Don't kick or splash while you swim.
- Don't block the shark's path.
- Back up against something. This is so sharks can't circle around you.
- Don't pee or bleed in the water.
- Roll into a ball. Do this if a shark is passing by you.
- Hit the shark in the gills, eyes, or snout. Only do this if you don't have any other choice.

BLOCK A OR BLOCK D?

It cost more to install the new steel bars than it cost to build the entire prison.

Before it was a prison, Alcatraz was a fort. It had over 100 cannons. It was built to look out all over the island. It had thick concrete walls. It had steel bars on the windows. These bars couldn't be cut. All of this made it hard to escape Alcatraz.

Cells are rooms. Each cell was like a prison inside a prison. Three of the cell walls were solid concrete. The front wall was made of steel bars. Only 1 inmate lived in each cell. Each cell had a bed, sink, toilet, and small desk. It had 2 small shelves.

Some inmates followed rules. Some inmates broke rules. Inmates were sent to different cell blocks based on their behavior.

QUESTION 2

Which cell block would you have stayed in?

A A-Block. Inmates stayed there while waiting for court. Or they stayed there while waiting to be transferred to another prison.

B B-Block or C-Block. Most inmates stayed there. They got 1 visitor per month.

C D-Block. This is where the worst inmates were housed. Inmates were punished there.

Inmates stayed by themselves for their first 3 months. They couldn't see visitors during this time either.

SURVIVAL BY THE NUMBERS

- Alcatraz housed about 250 to 275 inmates at a time. The prison had enough cells for 336 inmates.
- There's an "Escape from Alcatraz" contest. This event shows that with training and proper gear, people can swim from Alcatraz to the shore. It was first held in 1981. It includes a swim of 1.5 miles (2.4 kilometers). It includes a bike ride of 18 miles (29 km). It includes a run of 8 miles (13 km).
- There were 14 known attempts to escape from Alcatraz. These escapes involved 36 inmates: 23 inmates were captured, 6 were shot and killed, 2 drowned, and 5 went missing and are thought to have drowned.
- There was a prison battle from May 2 to May 4, 1946. During the battle, 6 inmates took weapons from **guards**. Guards watched over inmates. The inmates killed 2 guards. They harmed 18 guards. The U.S. Marines came. They ended the battle. Of the 6 inmates, 3 died. Of the remaining 3 inmates, 2 got the death penalty.
- On March 21, 1963, Alcatraz closed. It was open for 29 years. About $5 million was needed for repairs.

GOOD OR BAD?

The recreation yard was on raised land. It was surrounded by a high wall and fence.

Daily life in Alcatraz was tough. Inmates had to earn family visits. They had to earn activities. They could spend time in the **recreation** yard. Recreation means play. Inmates could play baseball or softball. They could play chess. They could talk to each other.

Inmates were punished for bad behavior. There were different types of punishments. Inmates had to wear heavy chains. They were kept in dark cells by themselves. They were fed only bread and water.

Inmates had one perk. They were allowed to take hot showers. This was to make them not want to escape. If inmates liked warm water, they'd hate the cold waters around Alcatraz.

QUESTION 3

What type of inmate would you have been?

A A good inmate. You followed all rules. Each morning, you cleaned your cell. You dressed. You got ready for head count. You ate meals. You worked. You went to bed when told.

B An okay inmate. You followed some rules. At times, you got punished. You got less time in the yard. You had to do hard **labor**. Labor is work.

C A bad inmate. You broke a lot of rules. You were sent to the Hole. The Hole was 5 cells in D-Block.

Alcatraz showed monthly movies. It also had a library with 15,000 books and 75 popular magazines. Inmates read 75 to 100 books a year.

SURVIVOR BIOGRAPHY

John Paul Scott lived from 1927 to 1987. He was an American criminal. He was born in Kentucky. He robbed a bank. He was sentenced to 30 years in prison. He went to Alcatraz in 1959. On December 16, 1962, he tried to escape from Alcatraz. He bent the bars of a bathroom window. He oiled himself with butter. He squeezed through the window bars. He climbed down a rope. He floated to the San Francisco shore. He had made water floats with stolen rubber gloves. He was the only Alcatraz escapee to reach the shore. But he passed out on the shore. He had **hypothermia**. Hypothermia is when your body loses heat. He was really tired. Four teens found him. They called the cops. Scott was taken to the hospital. Guards recaptured him quickly. They took him back to Alcatraz. After Alcatraz closed, Scott was sent to other prisons. He tried to escape. He was caught. He died in a Florida prison.

WORKER OR INMATE?

Workers lived in old fort barracks. Barracks are military rooms.

Inmates weren't the only ones living on Alcatraz Island. Many people worked at the prison. There was the warden. There were guards. They enforced rules. They punished inmates if needed. There was 1 guard for every 3 inmates.

People also worked in the kitchen. They worked in the laundry. They worked at the hospital. Inmates were assigned to work as well.

All workers lived on the island. Only men were hired. The workers' families lived there too. This included children. They lived in houses close to the prison.

QUESTION 4

Who would you have befriended at Alcatraz?

A A worker's child. Children took a boat to get off the island. This was how they went to school every day. They might have been able to help you escape.

B Other inmates. Having friends could have helped keep you safe.

C A warden or guard. Guards were highly trained in security. It would have been a risk, but they might have protected you.

Alcatraz started with 155 workers.

SURVIVAL TOOLS

Prison food is known to be bad. Ramen helps inmates survive. Ramen is instant noodles with a bag of spices. It's cheap. It has a lot of calories. It's available in prison stores. Inmates treat ramen like money. They trade ramen. They give ramen to people who do work for them. Second, they eat ramen. Ramen tastes better than prison food. Inmates get creative. They make many dishes. For example, they make "dirty ramen." This is ramen, Vienna sausages, green beans, and carrots. Another dish is made using ramen, mayonnaise, and Kool-Aid. A popular dish is called "chi chi" or "chee chee." This is made using ramen, chips, meat snacks, and sugar. Everything is put in a plastic bag. It's mixed up. It's put into a bowl of warm or hot water. It's covered with pillows and blankets. This is to hold heat.

GHOST OR NOT?

People reported seeing ghosts of Native Americans, soldiers, and inmates.

Alcatraz is one of California's most haunted spots. Inmates, guards, and visitors reported **sightings**. Sightings are reports of seeing something. They reported different ghostly events. They heard whispers at midnight. They heard moaning. They heard screaming. They heard clanking of chains. They heard women crying. They heard footsteps. They saw floating blue lights. They saw doors opening by themselves. They felt cold spots.

Some people say Al Capone's ghost is still at Alcatraz. He used to play the banjo in the shower. Banjo sounds were reported after Capone died. Some people said they felt Capone's fingers on the back on their neck.

QUESTION 5

Would you have believed Alcatraz is haunted?

A You didn't believe in ghosts. You could explain all the odd things. For example, whispers could be wind in the pipes.

B You weren't sure. You visited cell blocks A, B, and C. You heard crying and moaning.

C You believed it was haunted. D-Block is the most haunted. Cell 14-D was the worst. It was always cold. An inmate died in that cell. He reported seeing glowing red eyes.

Several ghost hunters investigated Alcatraz. One ghost hunter heard an evil spirit named Butcher. Butcher was an inmate at Alcatraz.

SURVIVAL RESULTS

Alcatraz held less than 1 percent of the total federal prison population. Federal means national government.

Would you have survived?

Find out! Add up your answers to the chapter questions. Did you have more **A**s, **B**s, or **C**s?

- If you had more **A**s, then you're a survivor! Congrats!

- If you had more **B**s, then you're on the edge. With some luck, you might have just made it.

- If you had more **C**s, then you wouldn't have survived.

Are you happy with your results? Did you have a tie? Sometimes fate is already decided for us. Follow the link below to our webpage. Scroll until you find the series name *Surviving History*. Click download. Print out the template. Follow the directions to create your own paper die. Read the book again. Roll the die to find your new answers. Did your fate change?

https://cherrylakepublishing.com/teaching_guides

DIGGING DEEPER: DID YOU KNOW...?

Alcatraz is a very interesting place. But prison life was tough. Surviving history involves many different factors. Dig deeper. Consider some of the facts below.

QUESTION 1:

Would you have tried to escape from Alcatraz?
- There were small bottom-feeding sharks around Alcatraz. There weren't many man-eating sharks in the waters.
- An escape requires a plane, boat, or long, hard swim.
- Inmates had no control over their diet. They had no control over physical activity.

QUESTION 2:

Which cell block would you have stayed in?
- A-Block held the offices. It was also used for storage. Inmates weren't held there for long.
- B-Block and C-Block cells were smaller than D-Block cells.
- D-Block was called the treatment block. Prisoners spent every minute in their cells. They had no contact with others. The cells had no lights. The walls were painted black.

QUESTION 3:

What type of inmate would you have been?
- Inmates who behaved could join one of several ball teams at Alcatraz.
- Inmates could only talk to each other during meals and yard time.
- Inmates in the Hole weren't allowed to have clothes. They didn't have a toilet.

QUESTION 4:

Who would you have befriended at Alcatraz?
- Children weren't allowed to have toy guns. Inmates could use toy guns to trick guards.
- Doctors didn't last long. They didn't like the violent inmates.
- Inmates and workers weren't allowed to talk to each other.

QUESTION 5:

Would you have believed Alcatraz is haunted?
- Alcatraz officials dismissed ghost sightings. They said these reports were nonsense.
- Mark Twain was a famous American writer. He said Alcatraz was "as cold as winter, even in the summer months." Some people think being cold is a sign of ghosts.
- People reported hearing gunfire, cannon blasts, and fire alarms.

GLOSSARY

barber (BAHR-bur) a person who cuts men's hair
cell blocks (SEL BLAHKS) prison housing units
cells (SELZ) rooms in a prison
criminals (KRIM-uh-nuhlz) people who break laws
currents (KUR-uhnts) strong waves
guards (GAHRDZ) officers who provide security services and enforce rules
hypothermia (HI-PO-ther-ME-a) when you lose heat faster than your body can make it
inmates (IN-mates) prisoners
labor (LAY-bur) work
maximum security (MAK-suh-muhm sih-KYOOR-ih-tee) having a high level of protection
mob boss (MAHB BAWS) head of a criminal group
recreation (rek-ree-AY-shuhn) play or leisure activity done for enjoyment
sightings (SITE-ingz) reports of seeing something
warden (WOR-duhn) the boss of a prison

LEARN MORE!

- Braun, Eric. *Escape from Alcatraz: The Mystery of the Three Men Who Escaped from the Rock*. North Mankato, MN: Capstone Press, 2017.
- Medina, Nico, and David Groff (illust.). *Where Is Alcatraz?* New York, NY: Grosset and Dunlap, 2016.
- Oliver, Marilyn Tower. *The Infamous Alcatraz Prison in United States History*. Berkeley Heights, NJ: Enslow Publishers Inc., 2015.

INDEX

A-Block, 14, 26, 30
Alcatraz, 4
  daily life, 17
  escape from, 10, 15, 19, 30
  history of, 13
  location, 9
  overview, 5, 7
  statistics, 15
  workers, 20–21, 31
B-Block, 14, 26, 30
Butcher, 27

C-Block, 14, 26, 30
Capone, Al, 5, 25

cell blocks, 7, 13, 14, 15, 30
children, 21, 22, 31
criminals, 5, 19
currents, 9, 10

D-Block, 14, 18, 26, 30

escapes, 5, 10, 15, 19, 30

food, 23
fort, 13

ghosts, 24–27, 31
guards, 21, 22

hard labor, 18

haunted places, 24–27, 31
Hole, the, 18, 31

inmates, 5, 6, 7, 13, 14, 15, 17, 18, 31

maximum security prison, 5
men, 21
museum, 4

prison, 5
punishments, 14, 17, 18

ramen, 23
recreation yard, 16, 17
Rock, the, 9

Scott, John Paul, 19
sharks, 9, 10, 11, 30
showers, hot, 17
steel bars, 12, 13
survival tips, 11

tools, survival, 23

"Uncle Sam's Devil's Island," 10

wardens, 7, 21, 22
workers, 20–21, 31

ABOUT THE AUTHOR

Dr. Virginia Loh-Hagan is an author, university professor, and former classroom teacher. She went to Angel Island, which is close to Alcatraz. She lives in San Diego with her very tall husband and very naughty dogs. To learn more about her, visit www.virginialoh.com.